Steam Memories: 1950's – 1960's

No. 96: Steam in the North

Tim Chapman

Copyright Book Law Publications 2017
ISBN 978-1-909625-76-1

INTRODUCTION

North West England was the last part of the country where British Rail used steam engines before their final demise in 1968. My pictures and notebook pages give detailed accounts of their use on particular days with the pictures in the precise order they were taken (apart from the very last page). Typically, for each train seen, as well as the locomotive number (of course), I recorded the type of train with origin and destination if known, the date and time of passing, the number of vehicles behind the locomotive, its approximate speed, direction, and headcode. The notes record what there was to see on some of the most interesting lines that the last steam trains ran on.

In addition to my own notes, many of my captions use information from British Rail Midland Region timetables and from Hugh Longworth's book "BR Steam Locomotives Complete Allocations History".

Dedication

First, to the memory of my late parents, Ken and Vera. Second, to the affection and patience of Carol, Louise and Edward who have enabled me to preserve some sanity whilst retrieving and organising pictures and records half a century old for presentation in the following pages.

Front Cover: 19th April 1968. Sporting handwritten smokebox engine numbers and 9H shedplates, Standard class 5s 73010 and 73134 pose in the sunshine outside their home shed Patricroft. Built at Derby in 1951, 73010 had been transferred to Patricroft from Oxley shed near Wolverhampton in 1965 and continued in use until June 1968. Also built at Derby but five years later, 73134 was one of thirty engines fitted with Caprotti valve gear out of a class total of 172. It went to Shrewsbury from new, was transferred to Patricroft in 1958 and stayed there until it too was withdrawn in June 1968.

Title page: An unidentified 9F 2-10-0, one of eight at Carnforth shed that day, stands next to the coaling tower on 26th August 1967. Carnforth was one of just three steam depots that remained open until August 1968, the month in which steam disappeared from the national rail network. The other two were Lostock Hall near Preston and Rose Grove near Burnley.

Printed and bound by The Amadeus Press, Cleckheaton, West Yorkshire
First published in the United Kingdom by Book Law Publications, 382 Carlton Hill, Nottingham, NG4 1JA

10th JULY 1965 — A SUMMER SATURDAY IN CARLISLE

The Railway Society of Darlington Queen Elizabeth Grammar School had organised our day trip. No steam for the journey there. English Electric type 4s took us to Newcastle on a York to Edinburgh service and from Newcastle to Carlisle on the Summer Saturdays Only Blackpool train. We headed off with our group permits for Kingmoor and Upperby sheds before taking our places on the platforms at Citadel station at 1pm. The photographs convey much of the day's action.

Enjoying sunshine that would be short lived, the crew of Kingmoor shed's black 5 No. 45135 watch the arrival of the eight coach 9am Newcastle to Blackpool train from which this photo was taken. With lifted safety valves showing the boiler to be at full pressure, 45135 looks ready to take the train southwards from Carlisle over Shap Summit to the seaside resort with stops at Oxenholme, Lancaster and Preston on the way. The walls of Citadel station can be seen behind the black 5's tender.

Britannia No. 70006, originally named *Robert Burns*, waits in line with a tender full of coal at Kingmoor depot as sunlight starts to fade. The lone figure was school teacher David MacKenzie who had the courage to lead our day's expedition from Darlington.

KINGMOOR (12A)
"Crab" 2-6-0 42863
Ivatt class 4 2-6-0 43004, 43028, 43121.
Stanier class 5 4-6-0
44668, 44692, 44715, 44720, 44796, 44798, 44802, 44884, 44898, 44899, 44901, 45061, 45120, 45126, 45140, 45163, 45195, 45221, 45258, 45259, 45337, 45473, 45474, 45491.
"Jubilee" 4-6-0 45588 Kashmir
45629 Straits Settlements 45742 Connaught
"Royal Scot" 4-6-0 46128 The Lovat Scouts
46160 Queen Victoria's Rifleman
"Jinty" 0-6-0 47305, 47471.
Stanier 8F 2-8-0 48536
"Britannia" 4-6-2
70006 Robert Burns, 70016 Ariel, 70036 Boadicea, 70038 Robin Hood.
"Clan" 4-6-2 72005 Clan Macgregor, 72006 Clan Mackenzie, 72008 Clan Macleod.
Standard Class 5 4-6-0 73007, 73079.
Standard Class 4 2-6-0 76049, 76063.
Standard Class 9 2-10-0 92010, 92130.
Diesel D5252, D5317.

UPPERBY (12B)
Ivatt class 2 2-6-2T 41285.
Fairburn 2-6-4T 42232.
Ivatt class 4 2-6-0 43017.
Fowler 4F 0-6-0 43953, 44081, 44390.
Stanier class 5 4-6-0
44761, 45141, 45083.
Ivatt class 2 2-6-0
46426, 46432, 46458, 46513.
"Jinty" 0-6-0 47667.
Stanier 8F 2-8-0 48406.
"Britannia" 4-6-2
70002 Geoffrey Chaucer,
70029 Shooting Star,
70044 Earl Haig, 70049 Solway Firth.
Diesel D215, D248, D278, D330.
Note: Diesel shunters not recorded.

TIME	LOCO(S)	TRAIN	VEH'S	CODE
NR	D248	Newcastle - Blackpool	8	1M54
13.00	70033->44761	Glasgow - Blackpool	9	
13.03	45660->70036	Birmingham - Glasgow	8	1S52
13.25	D269	Euston - Glasgow	13	
13.34	45081	Milk + parcels	31	
13.34	D1752	Glasgow - Manchester	12	1M29
13.38	45573-->?	CTAC Scot Tours Exp (D)	8	1S43
14.03	44670->44796	Blackpool - Edinburgh	10	1S54
14.08	DMU	D	5	
14.10	44887->70013	Glasgow (?) - Blackpool	10	1M12
14.??	DMU	Carlisle - Whitehaven	4	
14.30	70003	Hellifield - Carlisle	3	
14.45 ap	41222	Parcels+failed DMU->Upperby	3	
14.53	73009	Empty stock then LE (U)	3	
14.58	DMU	Newcastle - Carlisle	4	
15.05	D1842	The Mid-Day Scot (U)	12	1M35
15.18	D289	The Royal Scot(D)	12	
15.25	DMU	Carlisle - Whitehaven	2	
15.31	D268	Birmingham - Glasgow	13	
15.37	45573	LE from Kingmoor	0	1M97
15.41	D337	Perth - Euston	13	1M37
15.46	DMU	Carlisle - Newcastle	6	
15.48	DMU	Newcastle - Carlisle	4	
15.50	D1849	Birmingham - Edinburgh	10	1S62
15.58	D342	Euston - Perth	7	1S-3
15.58	D1837->45303	Glasgow (?) - Morecambe	10	1M32
16.06	41222	Empty stock from Upperby	9	
16.12/19	D22	The Waverley (D)	9	1S64
16.16	45185	Light engine	0	
16.22/30	73064->45573	CTAC Scot Tours Exp->S&C (U)	8	
16.28	D301	Passenger (D)	11	1S77
16.29	DMU	Carlisle - Newcastle	4	
16.41	45627	Glasgow(?) - L'pool/ Manch	11	
16.37	DMU	Carlisle - Whitehaven	4	
16.49	45185	Carlisle - Bradford F S	6	
17.00	D31	The Thames Clyde Express (D)	10	1S68
17.02	DMU	Newcastle - Carlisle	4	
17.15	DMU	Carlisle - Whitehaven	4	
17.25	D278	Light engine (D)	0	
17.29	DMU	Whitehaven - Carlisle	2	
17.31	DMU	Carlisle - Newcastle	4	
17.38	D373	Euston - Carlisle	6	1L25
17.42	DMU	Carlisle-Keswick-Workington	2	
17.45	D373	Light engine	0	3A09
17.48	D5312	Edinburgh - Carlisle	5	
18.02	DMU	Newcastle - Carlisle	4	
18.22/28	72007-	-D287 Stranraer - Newcastle	7	1N33

"Britannia" No. 70033 *Charles Dickens* waits in the centre road to head back to Kingmoor, its home depot, after arriving with a Glasgow to Blackpool train at 1 o'clock. Black 5 44761, seen previously at Upperby depot, sets off for the rest of the journey with the eight coach train.

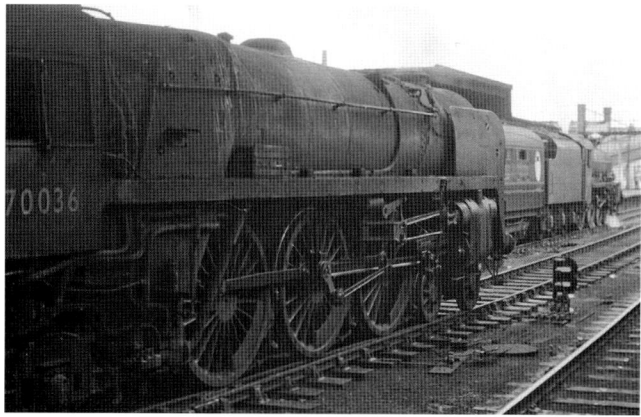

"Jubilee" 45660 *Rooke* arrived at 13.03 with a Birmingham to Glasgow service to be replaced by "Britannia" No. 70036, previously named *Boadicea*, for the onward journey. With eight coaches in tow, 70036 should not need a banking engine for the climb to Beattock summit.

5

"Jubilee" No. 45573 *Newfoundland* arrives from the West Coast main line with the *CTAC Scottish Tours Express* at 13.38. CTAC stood for Creative Tourist Agents Conference, a consortium of 9 UK travel agents and firms in North-West England which chartered special trains from 1933 to 1968, except during the war. 45573 was replaced here and took over the southbound working of this train at 16.22 (see page 7). With just two and three-quarter hours between its Citadel station appearances, one can speculate as to the destination and routes this train took in Scotland. Considering that Carlisle was a mecca for steam enthusiasts in 1965, it is surprising that there weren't more photographers and number collectors standing on the platform end on a summer Saturday.

With full pressure in the boiler, steam blasting out of its safety valves, and new coal on the fire, "Britannia" No. 70013 *Oliver Cromwell is* coupled to the 10 coach train to Blackpool before setting off at 14.10. The train had been brought into Citadel station from the north by black 5 44887 and had come from Dundee via Edinburgh and the Waverley route. *Oliver Cromwell* became a celebrity locomotive by hauling the last passenger train on British Rail tracks on 11 August 1968 and looks much smarter in its preserved condition than it did in this picture. After spending most of its British Railways life in East Anglia, it came to Carlisle Kingmoor depot in December 1963, though when this picture was taken it was based at Upperby shed. The Ivatt class 2 tank engine in the bay platform, No. 41222, was also an Upperby engine. Its duties that afternoon included hauling a failed DMU southwards out of the station and bringing empty stock back from the same direction.

"Jubilee" 45573 *Newfoundland* enters Citadel station from the north in the rain shortly after 4pm after being serviced at Kingmoor depot. It would later take over the CTAC Scottish Tours Express which it had also hauled northbound that same day (see page 6). *Newfoundland* spent its whole post war career based at Holbeck depot in Leeds. When it departed at 16.30 with the southbound working of the CTAC Scottish Tours Express, it headed towards the former Midland route over Ais Gill to Settle, Skipton and probably back to its home city. Sadly, the loco was nearing the end of its life and was withdrawn from service just two months later in September. D268 waits with a Birmingham to Glasgow train.

Postscript for the day in Carlisle

By July 1965 there were no Coronations or Princesses and the only Royal Scots were on Kingmoor shed. But a good few main line trains were still in the hands of steam with black 5s the most common class, and also Britannias, Jubilees, and standard class 5s. After the CTAC Scottish Tours Express, pictured above, diesels predominated apart from one Jubilee No. 45627 *Sierra Leone* on a Glasgow to Liverpool and Manchester train. And then a final treat. Our train back to Newcastle was a boat train from Stranraer and it came in behind "Clan" No. 72007 *Clan Mackintosh*. Carlisle was the end of the Clan's journey of course; we had to be content with propulsion across the Pennines by D287. I had for years assumed that the Clan would have come via Castle Douglas but in researching this book I discovered that that route had been closed less than a month before on 14 June. It would therefore have come the long way round via Ayr and Dumfries.

TUESDAY, 31st MAY 1966
AIS GILL TO DENTHEAD ON THE SETTLE – CARLISLE LINE

Steam was still working hard on the 1 in 100 gradients on the Settle to Carlisle. This was the first of several trips to record steam in the northern Pennines, though the line wasn't at its busiest that day. Our 11am arrival after a drive over Stainmore (the A66 was single carriageway in those days) meant that we could have missed the Long Meg to Runcorn anhydrite train, and from nearly 2pm to almost 4pm there was only one train - ballast wagons behind an Ivatt mogul that reversed at Dent, using the 2 hour gap for maintenance.

The last of the 55 "Britannias", No. 70054 previously named *Dornoch Firth* hauls a southbound 35 wagon freight train under the lofty bridge that carries Coal Road at the north end of Dent station. *Dornoch Firth* had been based at Carlisle Kingmoor depot just since January 1966 but would have seen regular use on the Settle to Carlisle line from 1958 to 1962 when it was shedded at Leeds Holbeck.

With a permanent way gang in attendance (no hi-viz jackets in those days!) Ivatt mogul 43049 waits on the down line at Dent station at the head of a dozen ballast wagons having come from the Garsdale direction and reversed over the crossover at the south end of the station. My notes state that the train went back towards Garsdale. The gang had nearly an hour to finish its work before getting out of the way of the next down train, the Thames-Clyde Express. The ballast train had been heading northwards at Mallerstang four hours earlier.

All is quiet at Dent station as 9F No. 92075 passes northwards with empty wagons from Widnes for the anhydrite traffic that originated at Long Meg sidings north of Appleby. This ten year old 9F spent most of its life based at the Nottinghamshire coalfield depots at Annesley, Toton and Kirkby in Ashfield before moving to Carlisle Kingmoor in March 1966. Its life there was short, withdrawal following in September of that year. This was the second of four northbound steam hauled freight trains that followed behind the Thames-Clyde Express that afternoon. Elaborate but poorly maintained snow fences can be seen on the hillside.

Black 5 No. 45437 heads downhill from Ais Gill summit with a 32 wagon freight train.

TIME	PLACE	LOCO	DIR	TRAIN	VEHICLES	HEADCODE	SPEED
10.58	Mallerstang	43XXX	D	Ballast freight (?)	13		20
11.50	Ais Gill summit	44983	U	Steel freight	19		25
12.00	Ais Gill summit	D30	D	Leeds - Glasgow	10	1S49	45
12.32	Garsdale station	D7599	D	Pigeon train	5	3X04	25
12.47	Garsdale station	D18	U	Express passenger	9	1M96	25
12.57	Garsdale station	DMU	D	Skipton-Carlisle	2		0
13.18	Dent station	D20	U	Thames-Clyde Express	12	1M86	65
13.39	Dent station	48473	D	Mixed freight	30		40
13.53	Dent station	70054	U	Mixed freight	35		35
14.49	Dent station	43049	U/D	Ballast freight	13		0
15.45	Denthead	44900	U	Mixed freight	35		45
15.56	Denthead	D23	D	Thames-Clyde Express	13	1S68	60
16.07	Denthead	75041	U	Mixed freight	19		40
16.13	Denthead	48745	D	Mixed freight	42		40
16.45	Dent station	92075	D	Empty mineral freight	25		40
17.40	Ais Gill summit	44854	D	Empty mineral freight	16		30
17.56	Ais Gill summit	DMU	D	Skipton-Carlisle	2		25
18.17	Ais Gill summit	DMU	U	Carlisle -Skipton	2		25
18.18	Ais Gill summit	45437	D	Mixed freight	32		30

TUESDAY, 20th SEPTEMBER 1966   AIS GILL, DENT AND RIBBLEHEAD

TIME	PLACE	LOCO	DIR	TRAIN	VEHICLES	HEADCODE	SPEED
11.11	Ais Gill summit	D1824	U	Glasgow-Manchester/Liverpool	11	1M27	35
11.21	Ais Gill summit	D1849	D	Road-railer freight	c28	3S35	45
11.23	Ais Gill summit	44853+92096	U	Long Meg-Widnes anhydrite			35
11.32	Ais Gill summit	D1617	D	Light engine	0	OE46	45
12.12	Ais Gill summit	D13	D	Leeds-Glasgow	8		40
c13.17	Dent station	D11	U	Thames-Clyde Express	11	1M86	50
13.23	Dent station	DMU	D	Shipton-Carlisle	2		0
13.26-35	Dent station	D1617		Light engine	0	OE46	0
13.34	Dent station	D1618	D	Express passenger	9	1S53	45
14.54	Ribblehead	44759	D	Mixed freight	38		30
15.00	Ribblehead	D27	D	The Waverley	8	1S64	5
15.35	Ribblehead	D35	UDU	The Waverley	7	1M91	0
16.07	Denthead	D17	D	Thames-Clyde Express	11	1S68	60
16.27	Dent station	43028	U	Rails freight	22		30
17.13	Dent station	D7557	U	Mixed freight	11	5M91	35
17.58	Dent station	DMU	D	Skipton-Carlisle	2		0
18.10	Dent station	92015	D	Widnes-Long Meg empties	23		35

A double headed Long Meg to Widnes anhydrite train climbs towards Ais Gill summit. Was there a problem with 9F 92096 or was black 5 44853 just working back to its home depot, 55A Holbeck, in Leeds?

SATURDAY, 1st OCTOBER 1966   TIMPERLEY

Viewed from Stoney Bridge Lane, off Park Road, in Timperley, 9F 92133 is approaching Skelton Junction with a mixed freight train from the Stockport direction. The right hand of three signals in the distance indicates that the train would take the southbound connection towards Altrincham and Northwich. After diverging to the right, this connection curved left and under the lines to Glazebrook and Warrington as it joined the electrified Manchester to Altrincham line. Black 5 No. 44868 on the eastbound line left its 35 wagons only to return light engine on the westbound line ten minutes later. It coupled on to the far end of its train and then shunted it into the loop line on the left of the picture until after another freight passed. The centre signal controlled traffic for the Glazebrook line which was closed between Partington and Glazebrook in 1982 and from Skelton Junction to Partington in 1993. On 28th March 2017, however, a scheme was launched to reopen the Skelton Junction to Glazebrook line as a heritage line with steam traction. The left hand signal was for the line to Warrington via Lymm. This closed in 1985 because of the high cost of maintaining Latchford viaduct over the Manchester Ship Canal. Most of it became part of route 62 of the National Cycle Network's Trans Pennine Trail.

TUESDAY, 4TH APRIL 1967   HELM TO KIRKBY STEPHEN

9F 92018 slogs up the 1 in 100 gradient near Grizeburn with an afternoon Long Meg to Widnes anhydrite train.

TIME	PLACE	LOCO	DIR	TRAIN	VEHICLES	HEADCODE	SPEED
10.10	Smardale	92114	U	Long Meg-Widnes anhydrite	21		30
12.04	Smardale	D35	D	Leeds-Glasgow	8	1S49	60
12.55	Shap station	D1583	U	The Royal Scot + mails	15	1M20	80
13.30	Shap troughs	D1957	U	Edinburgh-Birmingham	13		60
13.48	Shap troughs	D1847	U	Perth-London	11	1M26	60
14.00	Shap troughs	D1837	U	Light engine	0	0Z00	50
14.12	Shap troughs	D1632	D	The Royal Scot	12		45
14.56	Grizeburn	92018	U	Long Meg-Widnes anhydrite	21		15
15.24	Helm tunnel	44993	U	Carlisle-Skipton mixed freight	31		20
16.10	Helm tunnel	D29	D	The Thames-Clyde Express	11	1S68	65
17.21	Kirkby Stephen West	92051	D	Mixed freight	32		40
18.56a	Kirkby Stephen West	DMU	U	Carlisle-Skipton	2	B8	0
18.02	Kirkby Stephen West	DMU	D	Skipton-Carlisle	2	B8	0

MONDAY, 26TH JUNE 1967   GUIDE BRIDGE

Black 5 No. 44665 takes a 24 wagon freight train towards Manchester through the curved platforms at Guide Bridge. The main load was steel rods. It had just done a spell of shunting in the sidings on the south side of the electrified main line from Sheffield. These tracks and both curved platforms were abandoned in 1984/5 as the station's platforms were reduced from four to two.

After arriving from the Stockport direction, Northwich based Stanier 8F No. 48036 eases slowly away from Guide Bridge on the Woodhead tracks at the head of 48 empty mineral wagons. The loco would return as a light engine after 34 minutes, as recorded on page 17, presumably having left its wagons to an electric loco at the nearby Dewsnap sidings for the rest of the journey over Woodhead to the Yorkshire coalfield.

Stanier 8F No. 48321, with Newton Heath depot's 9D shedcode and assisted by another of the class, passes through Guide Bridge and slows for a signal stop at the head of 13 wagons, most of them carrying redundant track sections, before heading off towards Woodhead.

Shown on page 15 heading towards Woodhead, 8F No. 48036 appeared light engine from the Stalybridge direction having been turned, presumably using the triangle just east of the station. After a five minute wait to allow passage of the 17.00 Manchester Piccadilly to Marple DMU, the 8F headed off towards Stockport taking the track that curves left past the signal box. The tracks that curve off to the right led to Ashton-under-Lyne and connected with Miles Platting, Manchester Victoria and Oldham, though they did not seem to be in use that day.

SATURDAY, 1ST JULY 1967   KIRKBY STEPHEN, OXENHOLME AND SHAP

9F 92223 struggles to restart the Long Meg to Widnes anhydrite train after waiting in the up loop line at Kirkby Stephen to enable the 8.35 Carlisle to Skipton DMU to pass. 92223, like most of the engines seen working the anhydrite trains, was shedded at Carlisle Kingmoor at the time of the photograph. Only nine years old, it was based in the Western Region for its first five years and was not withdrawn until April 1968. The coal train in the down loop was hauled by Carnforth based 9F 92016.

TIME	PLACE	LOCO	DIR	TRAIN	VEHICLES	CODE	SPEED
9.56	Kirkby St'n W	DMU	U	Carlisle-Skipton	2		0(station)
10.07dep	Kirkby St'n W	92223	U	Long Meg-Widnes anhydrite	23		0(in loop)
10.08dep	Kirkby St'n W	92016	D	Coal freight	?		0(in loop)
10.41	Tebay	D1954	D	Liverpool-Glasgow/Edinburgh	11	1S46	70
10.52	Tebay	70046	U	Mixed freight	30		45
10.54	Tebay	D1956	D	Manchester-Glasgow/Edinburgh	12	1S45	70
11.06	Tebay	D1631	U	Carlisle-Euston	13	1M27	70
11.50	Grayrigg	45186	U	Newcastle-Blackpool (?)	6		50
11.50	Grayrigg	D1952	D	Euston-Perth	14		20
11.58	Grayrigg	45253	D	Vans freight	c40		35
12.10	Grayrigg	44873	D	Mixed freight	c30		25
12.47dep	Oxenholme	45445	D	Parcels to Windermere	2		0(station)
12.46/50	Oxenholme	DMU	U	from Windermere line	2		0(station)
12.56	Oxenholme	45435	U	Light engine	0		15
13.05	Oxenholme	D1953	U	The Royal Scot	11	1M20	60
13.10	Oxenholme	DMU	D	Empty stock	2	A0	20
13.45	Low Gill	D340	U	Edinburgh-Birmingham	12		60
14.01	Low Gill	D1635	U	Glasgow-Birmingham	12		45
14.06	Low Gill	75024	U	Light engine	0		50
c14.35	Scout Green	D1841	U	Glasgow-Liverpool	13		20
14.42	Scout Green	D1856	D	Birmingham-Glasgow	13	1S66	45
14.50	Scout Green	D359	D	Birmingham-Edinburgh	9		40
14.53	Scout Green	45227	U	Glasgow-Blackpool	11		25
15.01	Scout Green	70023	U	Edinburgh-Blackpool	11		20
15.07	Scout Green	44669	D	Mixed freight	20		25
12.09	Scout Green	45282	U	Soda Potash freight	12		20
15.15	Scout Green	D1852	U	Mixed freight	25		25
15.25	Scout Green	D315	D	Parcels	19		35
15.30	Scout Green	D1733	D	Manch'r/L'pool-Glas'/Edinb'	12	1P22	35
15.51	Scout Green	D1859	U	Glasgow-Euston	12		25
16.09	Scout Green	DMU	D	Carnforth-Carlisle	2		30
16.16	Scout Green	70011	D	D1854 being towed	1		40
16.22	Scout Green	92125	U	Mixed freight	43		20
16.41	Shap Wells	D1843	D	Euston-Perth	13	1S63	25
16.44	Shap Wells	D1846	U	Scotland-Euston	11		45
17.03	Shap Wells	70016	D	Euston-Carlisle	5		35
17.21	Shap summit	44905	U	Glasgow-Morecambe	10		35
17.28	Shap summit	70039	U	Glasgow-Liverpool	11		35
17.52	Shap summit	70025	D	Euston-Glasgow	8	1S80	30
18.28	Shap Wells	D1634	D	Euston-Glasgow	13	1S75	?
18.41	Shap Wells	D1948	U	Glasgow-Euston	9		45
19.18	Shap Wells	D1861	U	Car carrier	13		35
19.31	Shap Wells	D5708	U	Light engine	0		35
19.43	Shap Wells	D1631	D	Liverpool-Glasgow	13	1S76	35
c20.05	Shap Wells	D1847	U	Glas'/Edinb'-Manch'r/L'pool	12		40
20.10	Shap Wells	44842/75037	D	Mixed freight	25		25
20.16	Shap Wells	D1672	D	Vehicle delivery train	23	3S49	20
20.19	Shap Wells	Brush Type 4	U	Esso petrol freight	25		35
20.22	Shap Wells	Brush Type 4	D	Euston-Glasgow	9		30
21.14	Kirkby St'n W	44830	D	Empty mineral wagons	20		40

Standard class 4 4-6-0s await their next duties outside Tebay shed. The one further away was 75037 which had moved to Tebay from Stoke two months earlier and was seen that evening banking a black 5 hauled freight towards Shap summit (see page 24). Its stay was short, however. In December 1967 it was withdrawn before being scrapped in July 1968. The nearer one could have been 75024 which was seen during the afternoon heading away from Tebay at Low Gill. Eight members of this class were transferred to Tebay in April/May 1967 from either Stoke or Carnforth. Tebay shed closed in January 1968.

Seen from Docker Lane bridge, some five miles north of Oxenholme, and after ten miles of continuous uphill gradients, black 5 44873 makes steady progress towards Grayrigg with a Carlisle-bound freight that comprised some 30 wagons. The gradient here was 1 in 131 but the engine would have to keep working hard for the further three miles to the summit at Grayrigg, much of it at 1 in 106. 44873 had been a West Midlands based locomotive from nationalisation in 1948 until coming to the North-West in 1965. It was then looked after by the Wigan Springs Branch depot until withdrawal in December 1967.

Black 5 44659 makes a spirited ascent of the 1 in 75 gradient at Scout Green. There were two more miles to go before the gradient levelled out at Shap summit.

Steam to the rescue of a failed diesel! Britannia 70011 *Hotspur* **approaches Scout Green with Brush Type 4 D1854 in tow.**

Black 5 44905 coasts down from Shap summit through lineside clutter at Shap Wells with the summer Saturday 13.26 Glasgow to Morecambe service. This was the first of eight Saturdays that this train ran, the last one being on 19 August. It was scheduled to reach Morecambe Promenade station at 18.04 after making stops at Kilmarnock, Dumfries, Carlisle and Carnforth.

Following page. After Brush diesels had dominated early evening traffic, shortly after eight o'clock and in the best light of the day, a long freight was brought up past Shap Wells by black 5 44842. There was roughly one more mile of climbing at 1 in 75 to Shap summit. Assistance at the rear was given by Standard class 4 75037 which had been seen earlier outside Tebay shed (see page 20). It had been a quiet day for Tebay's banking engines.

24

WEDNESDAY, 5TH JULY 1967   PENRITH & SHAP

A rapidly changing scene. After shunting at Penrith, black 5 45481 heads off towards Keswick with a short freight. It is crossing the construction site of the Penrith bypass, opened sixteen months later in November 1968. This railway bridge is now located just north of junction 40 of the M6.

TIME	PLACE	LOCO	DIR	TRAIN	VEH	H'CODE	SPEED
09.28/33	Penrith	44993	U	Mixed freight	36		0(water)
9.41	South of Penrith	44805	U	Parcels and vans freight	44		25
9.45	South of Penrith	DMU	D	Carnforth-Carlisle	2		0(station)
9.52	South of Penrith	D1953	U	Glasgow-Euston	9	1M18	40
9.59	South of Penrith	45212	U	Mineral wagon empties	33		40
10.00	South of Penrith	D5708	D	Limestone freight	23		20
10.15	South of Penrith	Brush Type 4	D	Freightliner	16		45
10.15/29	South of Penrith	45481	U	Shunting, then freight-Keswick line	4		
10.42	South of Penrith	D1958	U	Glasgow-Manchester	13	1M27	50
10.42	South of Penrith	45089	D	Vans freight (on slow line)	43		10
10.45	South of Penrith	D1861	D	Passenger plus cars	12	1S41	50
10.58	South of Penrith	D1856	D	Liverpool-Glasgow/Edinburgh	c11	1S46	45
11.07	South of Penrith	D1958	D	Manchester-Glasgow/Edinburgh	11	1S45	45
12.04	Shap quarry	D1853	D	Birmingham-Perth	14	1S53	35
12.09	Shap quarry	D1845	D	Mixed freight	27	5P45	35
12.11 dep	Shap quarry	45212	D	Limestone freight from sidings	25		0(signal)
12.32	Shap quarry	45253	U	Mixed freight	c54		20
12.41	Shap quarry		D	Track testing machine			20
12.41	Shap quarry	D1843	U	The Royal Scot	11	1M20	30
12.56	Shap quarry	45349	U	Light engine	0		10
13.08	Shap quarry	D1956	U	Edinburgh-Birmingham	8	1M23	45
13.22	Shap quarry	D1690	U	Glasgow-Birmingham	12	1M24	45
13.33	Shap quarry	75030	U	Limestone freight	15		25
13.41	Shap quarry	D1949	U	Perth-Euston	11	1M26	c40
14.19	Shap summit	D1635	U	Glasgow-Manchester	11	1M29	10
14.21	Shap summit	D1840	D	The Royal Scot	12	1S57	45
14.38/46	Shap summit	44819/75039	DUD	Mixed freight	32		0
14.44/59	Shap summit	44918	U	Vans freight (took slow line)	54		0(signal)
14.45	Shap summit	D1645	D	Birmingham-Glasgow	12	1S61	45
15.07	Shap summit	D1623	D	Birmingham-Edinburgh	8	1S62	45
15.14/26	Shap summit	D1849	U	Cement freight (took slow line)	5	5A16	0(signal)
15.22	Shap summit	D1954	U	Perth-Birmingham	11	1M37	11
15.34d	Shap summit	75039	U	Light engine, Shap summit-Tebay	0		0
15.43	Shap summit	D1850	U	The Mid-Day Scot	11	1M35	15

A fourth black 5 at Penrith in an hour. No. 45089 waits in the down loop on the approach to Penrith with a 43 wagon freight. The home and distant signals are ready for one of three passenger trains headed by Brush Type 4 diesels that passed whilst the black 5 waited. The Keswick branch is visible behind the locomotive and the middle part of the train. It had closed between Keswick and Workington just over a year previously in April 1966 but on the day this photograph was taken there was still a service of seven passenger trains between Keswick and Carlisle. The section between Keswick and Penrith closed in 1972.

Black 5 44819 arrives at Shap summit with a 32 wagon mixed freight. It had been assisted by standard class 4 75039 up the 1 in 75 gradient from Tebay. 75039 stopped and 44819 continued a little further before reversing into the down siding to allow a Birmingham to Glasgow express to pass. The class 4 reversed onto the up main line and then into the up siding. It eventually left for Tebay 50 minutes after arrival, having waited for two up freights and the Perth-Euston passenger service. Shap summit was not one of the prettiest points on the West Coast Main Line's route through Westmorland.

After a 15 minute water stop in the up siding at Shap summit, black 5 44818 sets off down the 1 in 75 towards Tebay with a train comprising 54 vans. 44818 was built in Derby in 1944 and remained shedded in that town until the end of the 1950s. When this picture was taken it was shedded at Newton Heath where it had been based since 1963. It still had nearly a year's active life left before being withdrawn in June 1968 and scrapped the following December.

SATURDAY, 5TH AUGUST 1967
SKIPTON TO CARLISLE & OXENHOLME

Black 5 44802 stands ready to leave Oxenholme with the Saturdays Only Dundee to Blackpool train, scheduled to depart at 15.09. Prior to a quick dash under Oxenholme's subway to get this photo, I had travelled on this train on its non-stop journey from Carlisle. The black 5 had taken over from D358 which had brought it from Edinburgh over the Waverley route. Holiday trains originating in Scotland operated over a slightly earlier summer period than in England. This train ran from 24 June to 19 August and so would run just two more times after this day's journey. 44802 was based at Carlisle's Kingmoor shed. A week later it was used to haul freight on the Settle-Carlisle route (see page 37).

The 11.55 from Euston usually had steam haulage and more often than not it would be a "Britannia". Maybe the smaller tractive effort of black 5 45227 was part of the reason for the train's fifty minute late arrival at Oxenholme, where the coaches were divided into portions for Carlisle and Windermere. The 11.55 ran Saturdays Only from the start of the summer timetable on 17 June until 26 August. Before Oxenholme it had timetabled stops at Crewe, Warrington Bank Quay, Wigan North Western, Preston and Lancaster Castle.

Black 5 45227 rests at the north end of Carlisle Citadel station having arrived in early evening sunshine at the head of the 11.55 from Euston with the author as one of its passengers. The service was due to arrive at 17.39 after making one further intermediate stop at Penrith. Fortunately for me, the black 5 must have avoided losing further time after the late departure from Oxenholme. I was able to catch the evening Glasgow to Leeds train, due to depart Carlisle at 18.41, for my return over the Settle Carlisle route back to Skipton. 45227 was a regular on the West Coast Main Line; Lostock Hall shed near Preston was its home depot at the time of the photograph and before that Carnforth had been its home depot. It continued in service until January 1968.

TIME	PLACE	LOCO	DIR	TRAIN	VEH	CODE	SPEED
11.12	Skipton	44912	U	Parcels	5		0 (station)
11.17/19	Skipton	D5256	D	Leeds-Morecambe	8	1M05	0 (station)
11.23/30	Skipton	D13	D	Leeds-Glasgow	13	1S43	0 (station)
11.23	Skipton	75042	D	Limestone freight	13		5
11.33/38	*Skipton (to Carlisle)*	*45562*	*D*	*Birmingham-Glasgow*	*8*		*0 (station)*
11.35	Skipton	45089	U	Light engine	0		10
11.51	South of Hellifield	44983	U	Morecambe-Bradford	?		c45
12.00	Hellifield	45198	U	Vans freight	?		0
12.00	Hellifield	92071+92125	D	Rails freight	?		0
12.16	Horton in Ribblesdale	44943	U	Freight	5		0
	Carlisle Citadel	45562/70028	D	Birmingham-Glasgow	8		0 (station)
13.50a	Carlisle Citadel	45297	D	Blackpool-Dundee	10		0 (station)
13.57d	Carlisle Citadel	44911	U	Glasgow-Blackpool	9		0 (station)
14.08d	*Carlisle (to Oxenholme)*	*D358/44802*	*U*	*Dundee-Blackpool*	*9*		*0 (station)*
14.11	Upperby sidings	45135	U	Soda Ash freight	?		0 (signal)
14.25	Southwaite loop	44767	U	Mixed freight	?		0 (signal)
14.40	Near Penrith	45221	D	Passenger	?		c60
15.31	Grayrigg bank	44778	D	Light engine	0		?
16.12	Oxenholme	D221	U	Glasgow-Birmingham	10		75
16.20	Oxenholme	D1854	U	Glasgow-Euston	12	1M35	70
16.30/32	Oxenholme	D1632	U	Windermere-Euston	?		0 (station)
16.37	Oxenholme	D1621	D	Euston-Glasgow/Perth	13	1S63	60
16.39	Oxenholme	44767	U	Mixed freight	42		35
16.47	Oxenholme	45135	U	Soda Ash freight	13		25
16.53	Oxenholme	D1625	U	Mixed freight	40	5A16	20
17.00	Oxenholme	D1823	U	Freightliner	16	3M35	30
17.12/26	*Oxenholme (to Carlisle)*	*45227*	*D*	*Euston-Carlisle/Windermere*	*11 then 5*	*..2.*	*0 (station)*
17.26	Oxenholme	70014	U	Glasgow/Edinb'-Manch'r/L'pool	c10		c50
18.34/42	*Carlisle (to Leeds)*	*D17*	*U*	*Glasgow-Leeds*	*13*	*1N63*	*0 (station)*
18.44	Carlisle goods	92071+92125	D	Rails freight	?		20
18.45	*Petteril Bridge*	92021	*D*	Mixed freight	44		20
20.15	Settle Junction	D5254	U	Morecambe-Leeds	8	1N71	0 (signal)

SATURDAY, 12TH AUGUST 1967
KIRKBY STEPHEN AND AROUND AIS GILL SUMMIT

Just one year before steam would be completely eliminated from standard gauge British Railways.

9F 92110 makes steady but slow progress up the 1 in 100 gradient towards Birkett Tunnel on the southbound climb towards Ais Gill summit. This viewpoint was a mile to the south of Kirkby Stephen where Wharton Lane crosses under the tracks. As happened six weeks earlier (see page 18), the Long Meg to Widnes anhydrite train had stopped at Kirkby Stephen. I could hear it restarting from this viewpoint. It had struggled to accelerate its 20 wagons to all of 15 miles per hour as it passed but was a sight to behold as it laboured across the embankments on its approach with the Vale of Eden as the backdrop.

After passing Wharton Lane in the previous picture, it took 9F 92110 a further 26 minutes to climb the last five miles mainly at 1 in 100 to Ais Gill summit, proving that my notebook estimate of 10 mph for its speed there was not far off. Even my Dad's Farina styled Morris Oxford could beat that time to the summit, despite the longer route back down the A685 to Kirkby Stephen and along the B6259 up the Eden valley past Mallerstang. I watched the 9F's slow progress along the lower slopes of Wild Boar Fell overtaking it in time to park and photograph its volcanic breasting of the summit.

The next up train after the anhydrite train from Long Meg over Ais Gill summit was also steam hauled. It comprised 35 empty hopper wagons plus the guard's van behind black 5 44943 which maintained a fine smoke display for the early part of its southward descent on the gentler gradients towards Garsdale. 44943 was allocated to Leeds Holbeck shed for all of its post- war life apart from a three year stint just a mile away at Farnley Junction depot from 1963 to 1966. Its safety valve indicates that its boiler must have been steaming well on the long climb from Appleby to Ais Gill. This did not, however, save it from an early fate; it was withdrawn in September 1967 just two months after this picture was taken.

Facing page. With the slopes of Mallerstang Common rising above the tracks, black 5 44802 descends from Ais Gill summit with empty hopper wagons, possibly returning from Widnes to Long Meg sidings for the next trainload of anhydrite.

TIME	PLACE	LOCO	DIR	TRAIN	VEHICLES	H'CODE	SPEED
9.55	Kirkby Stephen	DMU	U	Carlisle-Skipton	2		0 (station)
9.56	Kirkby Stephen	D37	U	Mixed freight	25	5M-6	0 (signal)
10.52	North of Birkett Fell	92110	U	Long Meg-Widnes anhydrite	21		15
11.18	Ais Gill summit	92110	U	Long Meg-Widnes anhydrite	21		10
12.06	Ais Gill summit	D29	D	Leeds-Glasgow	12	1S49	40
12.12	Ais Gill summit	44943	U	Empty hopper wagons	36		20
12.17	Ais Gill summit	45562	D	Birmingham-Glasgow	8		40
12.37	Shotlock Tunnel	D397	U	Glasgow-St. Pancras	?	1M85	50
12.57	Shotlock Tunnel	45259	D	Vans freight	45		30
13.05	Shotlock Tunnel	DMU	D	Skipton-Carlisle	2		35
13.15	Shotlock Tunnel	D34	U	The Thames-Clyde Express	12	1M86	45
13.22	Shotlock Tunnel	48517+92137	D	Rails freight	24		30
13.35	Shotlock Tunnel	D1838	U	Passenger	6	1Z24	45
14.08	Ais Gill summit	44802	D	Empty hopper wagons	c23		30
14.49	Ais Gill summit	D190	D	The Waverley	8		45
14.52	Ais Gill summit	44886	U	Freight	3		40
15.07	Ais Gill summit	45562	U	Light engine	0		35
15.27	Shotlock Tunnel	D15	U	The Waverley	9	1M91	60
15.59	Shotlock Tunnel	45593	D	St. Pancras-Glasgow	8		40
16.09	Shotlock Tunnel	D73	D	The Thames-Clyde Express	10	1S68	40

Compared to the other steam hauled freights that day, the fireman of black 5 44886 would have had little trouble raising steam for this short load of hydrated lime containers, seen here approaching Ais Gill summit. The bridge carries the B6259 road that links Kirkby Stephen with Garsdale and Wensleydale. The hill on the left is Lunds Fell and the one in the distance is Widdale Fell. Ais Gill was on the watershed of England. North of the summit the streams formed the headwaters of the River Eden flowing into the Irish Sea via Solway Firth. South of the summit they drained to the Rivers Ure and Ouse reaching the North Sea via the Humber estuary.

"Jubilee" 45562 *Alberta* heads towards Ais Gill summit on its return to Leeds having hauled the 6.40 Birmingham-Glasgow train from there to Carlisle earlier in the day. This was a curious train which left Leeds at 10.17 with intermediate stops at Keighley, Skipton and Appleby en route to Carlisle. It then took the former Glasgow and South Western Railway's route into Scotland via Kilmarnock with a further four stops before its Glasgow arrival at 15.55. With an overall scheduled time of nine hours and fifteen minutes, more than three hours longer than the service via Crewe, there must have been few if any passengers that would have made the full journey from Birmingham! On Mondays to Fridays in the summer, the 6.40 from Birmingham went just as far as Leeds. It ran on to Glasgow just on Saturdays from 15 July to 26 August. On most if not all of these summer Saturdays the train was hauled by *Alberta* or by Holbeck shed's other "Jubilee" 45593 *Kolhapur.*

"Jubilee" 45593 *Kolhapur* bursts out of Shotlock Tunnel on the final leg of its climb to Ais Gill summit with the summer Saturday 9.20 St. Pancras to Glasgow. This train ran from 15 July to 26 August running just ahead of the Thames-Clyde Express, collecting passengers at seven stations on the Midland Main Line that the Thames-Clyde missed and going via Derby instead of Nottingham. With a non-stop run from Leeds to Carlisle, it was the fastest northbound train of the day between these two cities and was a regular steam turn! Kolhapur was a Carlisle Upperby engine from 1951 to 1961. After leaving Carlisle it had briefer stays at Willesden, Aston, Burton, Patricroft and Newton Heath before moving to Leeds's Holbeck depot on 23rd March 1965. It became a regular performer between Leeds and Carlisle line until its eventual withdrawal in October 1967. It was purchased by the Standard Gauge Steam Trust a year later and at the time of writing was awaiting overhaul at Tyseley Locomotive Works.

SATURDAY, 19TH AUGUST 1967 LANCASTER TO CARLISLE AND BACK

The nine coach summer Saturdays Only 10.45 Blackpool North to Dundee train arrives at Shap Summit behind black 5 No. 44915 and stops to detach pilot locomotive Standard class 4 No. 75040 which had given assistance from Oxenholme. The Standard crossed to the up main line at the summit prior to returning to its home depot at Carnforth.

At Carlisle Citadel station, black 5 No. 45285 waits to depart with the 09.10 Dundee to Blackpool train which had been brought over the Waverley route from Edinburgh by English Electric type 4 diesel D363. 45285 had been based at Kentish Town depot in London right through the 1950s. It then had several homes before coming to Carlisle's Kingmoor depot in June 1967 only to be withdrawn in the following December.

TIME	PLACE	LOCO	DIR	TRAIN	VEHICLES	H'CODE
11.50	Lancaster Castle	44874	D	Light engine	0	
12.06	*Lancaster Castle (to Carlisle)*	*44915*	*D*	*Blackpool-Dundee*	*9*	*1S54*
12.27	North of Milnthorpe	45001	U	Guards van	1	
?	Oxenholme (to Shap)	75040	D	*Blackpool-Dundee pilot*		
13.03	Grayrigg	45435	U	*Light engine*	0	
13.12	Scout Green	75024	U	Light engine	0	
13.19	Shap summit	48703	U	Light engine (with snowplough)	0	
		D363				
13.53/14.00	Carlisle Citadel	45285	U	Dundee-Blackpool	9	1M31
14.26	Carlisle Citadel	D1972	U	The Waverley	8	1M91
15.41	Carlisle freight loop	44915	U	Light engine	0	
16.11 dep	Carlisle Citadel	D1851	U	Freightliner	16	3M35
16.14 dep	Carlisle Citadel	45349	U	Glasgow-Morecambe	9	
16.29	*Carlisle Citadel (to Lancaster)*	*70051*	*U*	*Glasgow/Edinburgh-Manchester/Liverpool*	*12*	

Travelling tender first, black 5 No. 44915 approaches the Currock Road overbridge in Carlisle on the Citadel station avoiding line. It had come from the north end of Carlisle where the avoiding line diverged from the main line about half a mile from Citadel station. The tracks to the left were the start of the link to the coast route to Whitehaven and Barrow, joining the lines from Citadel station after rather less than half a mile. The junction in the picture was the eastern end of a triangle that enabled traffic from the coast route to also avoid Citadel station. The signals at the top of the picture indicate the choice of three routes available to the driver. Just after the overbridge, branching right led to the West Coast Main Line and Upperby depot; the straight on lines joined the lines from Citadel station to Newcastle and Leeds. The tracks under the black 5 were closed after the River Caldew bridge just north of this triangle was damaged by runaway container wagons. The lines to the coast route in the picture, however, were still in place in 2016.

The 13.26 Glasgow to Morecambe train ran for the last time on 19 August, the service having started on 1st July. The beautifully presented black 5 No. 45349 which took control of the train at Carlisle Citadel had been shedded at Crewe South since November 1966 so was at the fringes of its usual territory on this day. In front of the locomotive on the lower picture, the tracks going down the gradient go to Newcastle and Leeds, the centre tracks are the West Coast Main Line, and the tracks curving to the right are the start of the coast line to Whitehaven and Barrow.

With the mountains of the Lake District's High Street range behind the engine and signals, "Britannia" 70051 Firth of Forth accelerates away from its 16.52 Penrith stop with the 14.00 from Glasgow / 14.10 from Edinburgh to Manchester and Liverpool. This train ran on Fridays and Saturdays from 17th June to 2nd September with further stops at Oxenholme, Carnforth, Lancaster and Preston. The tracks on the right led to the Keswick branch.

SATURDAY, 26TH AUGUST 1967   LEEDS TO CARLISLE AND CARNFORTH

The 6.40 Birmingham to Glasgow train (depart Leeds 10.17) was booked to stop at Skipton from 10.56 to 11.12 to allow the 10.25 Leeds to Glasgow to overtake it. The 16 minute stop gave photographers plenty of time to record the scene and for the crew to pose for the cameras. Leeds Holbeck shed's "Jubilee" 45562 *Alberta* had become a regular on this train which could be depended on for steam haulage over the Settle – Carlisle line in the summer of 1967.

The 6.40 Birmingham to Glasgow passes under Carleton New Road as it sets off from Skipton behind "Jubilee" 45562 *Alberta*. Skipton was *Alberta's* second intermediate stop after taking charge of the train at Leeds, Keighley being the first, and it made one further stop at Appleby West. At Carlisle, "Britannia" 70028 Royal Star took the train on to Glasgow Central with more stops at Annan, Dumfries, Kirkconnel and Kilmarnock. After being a Leeds based engine for all of its post war life, *Alberta* was withdrawn from service in November 1967 and cut up at Cashmore's yard at Great Bridge near Tipton in the West Midlands the following May. Trains from Ilkley and Grassington used the lines on the left of the picture. The Ilkley to Skipton Line had closed in March 1965 just over two years before this picture was taken, though its intermediate stations at Embsay and Bolton Abbey have been reconnected by the Embsay Steam Railway. Limestone trains still use the Grassington branch to and from Swinden Quarry.

Seen from St. Nicholas Bridge over the Citadel station avoiding line, black 5 No. 45279 heads southwards out of Carlisle towards Penrith with the 11.05 summer Saturdays only Glasgow to Blackpool service.

TIME	PLACE	LOCO	DIR	TRAIN	VEHICLES	H'CODE
10.10	Leeds City	45080		Passenger	?	
10.22 dep	*Leeds City (to Carlisle)*	*45562*	*D*	*Birmingham-Glasgow*	*8*	
10.57	before Silsden & Steeton	44826	U	Mixed freight	?	
11.11/16	Skipton	D23	D	Leeds-Glasgow	11	1S49
11.37	Hellifield	45219	U	Morecambe-Bradford	8	
11.40	N of Hellifield	92004	U	Hopper wagons freight	?	
c13.50	S of Carlisle Citadel	45279	U	Glasgow-Blackpool	9	
14.15	S of Carlisle Citadel	70035	D	Light engine	0	
14.27	S of Carlisle Citadel	DMU	D	Middlesbrough-Carlisle (football special)	12	
14.28	S of Carlisle Citadel	D32	U	The Waverley	8	
14.40	S of Carlisle Citadel	D1957	D	The Royal Scot	13	1S57
14.41	S of Carlisle Citadel	D1841	U	Glasgow-Birmingham	10	1M37
15.06	S of Carlisle Citadel	D1860	U	Glasgow-Euston	11	1M35
15.15	S of Carlisle Citadel	D1621	D	Birmingham-Glasgow	12	1S61
c15.30	S of Carlisle Citadel	D1623	D	Birmingham-Edinburgh	10	1S62
15.45	S of Carlisle Citadel	D22	D	The Waverley	8	1S64
16.26 dep	*Carlisle Citadel (to Carnforth)*	*70039*	*U*	*Glasgow/Edinburgh-Manchester/Liverpool*	*11*	
16.52	Penrith	45285	D	Parcels	?	
17.15	Shap quarry	44993	D	Euston-Carlisle	c5	
17.36	Oxenholme	44711	D	Euston-Glasgow	10	
17.52	S of Milnthorpe	70004	D	Parcels	?	
18.06	Carnforth	D5108	D	Blackpool-Newcastle	8	
19.10/12	*Carnforth (to Leeds)*	*D7549*	*D*	*Morecambe-Leeds*	*6*	
19.56	Hellifield	45013	D	Empty hopper wagons freight	?	

Steam hauled expresses pass at Oxenholme. Whilst the 14.00 from Glasgow / 14.10 from Edinburgh to Manchester and Liverpool behind "Britannia" 70039 *Sir Christopher Wren* was waiting to leave the up platform, black 5 No. 44711 rushes in to the station with the 13.20 Euston to Glasgow service. This latter train operated from 1st July until the end of the summer Saturday timetable on 2nd September, running non-stop between Crewe and Carlisle. The "Britannia" must have been on good form. In the timetable, it had a two minute stop but when the picture was taken it still had eight minutes to wait before its scheduled 17.44 departure. The black 5 is approaching a pair of banner repeater signals. The diagonal banner on the higher signal confirms that the train is heading straight on for the main line towards Carlisle. The lower signal would be set at diagonal for trains taking the branch line to Windermere.

With steam to spare, "Britannia" 70039 Sir Christopher Wren sets off from Carnforth with the 14.00 from Glasgow (and 14.10 from Edinburgh) to Manchester and Liverpool.

LOCOMOTIVES AT CARNFORTH SHED (10A) ON 26th AUGUST 1967

Fairburn class 4 2-6-4T
42210
Ivatt class 4 2-6-0
43105
Stanier class 5 4-6-0
44667, 44709, 44715, 44733, 44758,
44778, 44780, 44825, 44838, 44874,
44889, 44892, 44894, 44897, 44905,
44948, 44963, 44971, 45001, 45014,
45017, 45025, 45072, 45095, 45149,
45193, 45253, 45254, 45342, 45374,
45394, 45424, 45435.
"Jubilee" 4-6-0
45697 Achilles

Ivatt class 2 2-6-0
46400, 46431, 46433, 46499.
Stanier 8F 2-8-0
48061, 48441, 48666.
"Britannia" 4-6-2
70010 Owen Glendower, 70027 Rising Star.
Standard Class 4 2-6-0
75009, 75010, 75020, 75021, 75024,
75033, 75040, 75041, 75042, 75043,
75048, 75058, 75059, 75062.
Standard Class 9 2-10-0
92016, 92055, 92071, 92118, 92126,
92128, 92212, 92223.
Diesel
D2116, D2392, D3008, D3200, D3286,
D3566, D4142, D4139, D5256, D5718.

The crew watch carefully as they reverse "Britannia" 70010 past the coaling plant at Carnforth shed. 70010's missing metal nameplate had been "*Owen Glendower*", an anglicised spelling of the leader of a rebellion against Henry IV in 1400. Its handwritten name in the picture, however, was "Owain Glyndwr", a spelling more likely to find favour in Wales! No fewer than seventy one steam locos were on Carnforth shed that day – thirty three of them black 5s. Its change of shed code in 1963 from 24L to 10A reflected its rise in importance as steam use declined in the region. The coaling plant was listed at Grade II for its special historic interest in 1989 for the following reasons, to quote Historic England:

"Technology: the plant represents the peak of technological development for the refuelling of steam locomotives; Rarity: the only steam-age mechanical coaling plant retaining its mechanism that survives nationally, also thought to be a rare survival internationally; Efficiency: the London Midland Scottish Railway led the way nationally in improving operating efficiency and developed an ultra-efficient design for their Motive Power Depots, these representing the peak of development for steam traction, the coaling plant being an important, high-tech component of the depot; Distinctiveness: the widely known and modelled structure that marks the high point of steam technology, being the most memorable feature of the last British Rail depot to close to steam locomotives; Group value: part of a remarkably complete survival of a steam-age Motive Power Depot."

SATURDAY, 2ND SEPTEMBER 1967   KIRKBY STEPHEN, TEBAY AND SHAP

This page and facing page. Having stopped just north of Tebay station to have a banking engine attached, black 5 45295 heads off again to tackle the climb to Shap summit with a long mixed freight train. The banking engine's smoke is visible in the distance on this page. Apart from two brief interludes at Stoke and Edge Hill, 45295 was based at Carlisle Upperby depot for all its post war life until June 1963, after which it saw out its final years at Kingmoor until withdrawal in December 1967.

This page and previous page. Departing Tebay at 12.30, this was the second of three banked freights on 2nd September, all within 90 minutes of each other. The assistance for black 5 45295 was given by Tebay shed's Standard Class 4 No. 75039 performing during its last month of service before withdrawal.

This page and facing page. The last of three banked freights had a "Britannia" in charge, No. 70021 *Morning Star*, with 75037 banking at the rear. Again, the banking engine's smoke can be seen in the distance. *Morning Star* was a much travelled locomotive having been based in Devon, Cardiff, Birmingham, Manchester and Crewe before coming to Carlisle Kingmoor in June 1967. The scene here has been changed drastically by the M6 which crosses over the railway near to where the train goes out of the picture. It crosses the River Lune this side of the pedestrian bridge at its junction 38 with the A685.

This page and previous page. Standard class 4 No. 75037 banks *Morning Star's* freight train away from Tebay near the start of the five mile climb to Shap summit. Though this was the fiercest climb on the West Coast Main Line, with four miles at 1 in 75, the gradient at Tebay station and the next mile or so was less severe at 1 in 146, giving trains that needed to stop for a banker a chance to get going before maximum effort was needed.

TIME	PLACE	LOCO	DIR	TRAIN	VEH	H'CODE	SPEED
9.20	Kirkby Stephen	D145	U	Mixed freight	18		25
9.38	Kirkby Stephen	92017	U	Long Meg-Widnes anhydrite	21		15
11.12	Greenholme	D1616	U	Carlisle-Euston	12	1M27	75
11.13	Greenholme	44678/75037	D	Mixed freight	c25		15
11.35	North of Tebay	75037	U	Light engine	0		0 (signal)
12.04	North of Tebay	D1855	D	Birmingham-Perth	12		65
12.07	North of Tebay	44677	U	Mixed freight	41		25
12.14	North of Tebay	D7677	D	Light engine	0	0Z00	50
12.23	North of Tebay	92233	U	Mixed freight	43		35
12.32	North of Tebay	45295/75039	D	Mixed freight	c35		20
12.35	North of Tebay	D1620	D	Mixed freight	42	5P45	40
12.47	North of Tebay	70021/75037	D	Mixed freight	?		0 (signal)
c13.05	Shap Wells	75039	U	Light engine	0		NR
13.10	Shap Wells	75037	U	Light engine	0		NR
15.15	Shap Wells	D1623	D	Birmingham-Edinburgh	10	1S62	c30
15.21	Shap Wells	D1804	U	Mixed freight	25		c45
15.37	Shap Wells	D223	U	Aberdeen-Birmingham	10		c55
15.42	Shap Wells	D1959	U	Glasgow-London	11		60
15.56	Shap Wells	D1954	D	Manchester-Glasgow	11	1S71	40
16.20	Shap Wells	DMU	D	Carnforth-Carlisle	2		25
16.25	Shap Wells	D289	D	Parcels	23		30
16.43	Shap quarry	D1845?	U	Freightliner	15	3M55	c40
16.52	Shap quarry	D1635	D	Euston-Glasgow	8		35
17.11	Shap quarry	D1844	U	Glasgow/Edinburgh-Manchester/Liverpool	11	1M38	45
17.59	Shap Wells	70025	D	Euston-Glasgow	8		35
18.34	Scout Green	D1952	D	Euston-Glasgow	13	1S75	40

Steam enthusiasts' faces peer from the windows of the last 1967 run of the summer Saturdays Only 13.20 Euston to Glasgow as it passes Shap Wells. With safety valves indicating full boiler pressure despite having already climbed three miles at 1 in 75, "Britannia" 70025 *Western Star* was making a spirited climb towards Shap summit in the fine early evening sunshine. Passing here at 6 o'clock, the "Britannia" had been running for two and a half hours since its timetabled departure from Crewe on the scheduled non-stop run to Carlisle.

WEDNESDAY, 27TH SEPTEMBER 1967   SHAP AND THRIMBY GRANGE

Twenty five days after the picture on the previous page, "Britannia" 70025 *Western Star* still looks to be steaming freely with its safety valves lifting despite the long climb to Shap summit from Carlisle. Here it is again at Shap Wells but this time freewheeling downhill towards Tebay with a 46 wagon mixed freight. Western Star had been transferred from Crewe to Carlisle Kingmoor depot in 1966 where it stayed until being withdrawn in December 1967. All but 5 of the 55 "Britannias" ended their days at Carlisle, and only 70013 Oliver Cromwell survived into 1968.

TIME	PLACE	LOCO	DIR	TRAIN	VEHICLES	H'CODE	SPEED
10.17	Shap Wells	44759	U	Mixed freight	36		45
10.22	Shap Wells	D338	U	Mixed freight	40		40
10.27	Shap Wells	70004	D	Parcels	6		30
10.36	Shap Wells	70025	U	Mixed freight	46		45
10.53	Shap summit	D1804	D	Vans freight	55	5P44	20
11.07	Shap summit	D1826	U	Carlisle-Euston	12	1M27	45
11.08	Shap summit	D1859	D	Manchester-Glasgow/Edinburgh	12	1S45	30
11.26	Shap summit	45279	U	Empty rail wagons	c30		35
11.36	Shap summit	D1841	D	Mixed freight	54	5P45	20
11.54	Shap summit	D1858	D	Birmingham-Perth	7	1S53	50
12.17	Shap summit	92122	U	Mixed freight	42		40
12.25	Shap summit	92XXX	U	Freight			25
12.43	Shap summit	Brush type 4	U	The Royal Scot	11		45
13.40	Shap Wells	Brush type 4	U	Perth-Euston	10		
13.46	Shap Wells	48735/75032	D	Mixed freight	c40		
14.25	Thrimby Grange	Brush type 4	U	Metropolitan Vickers Co-Bo diesels	2		c30
14.53	Thrimby Grange	Brush type 4	D	Birmingham-Perth	12	1S61	60
15.02	Thrimby Grange	44886	U	Mixed freight	24		20
15.05	Thrimby Grange	D307	U	Passenger	8		60
15.12	Thrimby Grange	D1632	U	Perth-Birmingham	8		45
15.17	Thrimby Grange	D1804	U	Mixed freight	c40		25
15.23	Thrimby Grange	92055	D	Mixed freight	48		45
15.40	Thrimby Grange	D382	U	Glasgow-Euston	11	1M35	35
16.24	Thrimby Grange	DMU	D	Carnforth-Carlisle	4		45
16.44	Little Strickland	D1854	D	Euston-Perth	12	1S63	60
17.06	Little Strickland	D1841	U	Vans freight	37	5K15	40
18.30	Shap Wells	92XXX/75032	D	Freight			15

During the early afternoon, Standard class 4 75032 banks a long mixed freight train up the 1 in 75 gradient at Shap Wells. Stanier 8F 48735 was at the head of the train. 75032 would also assist a 9F that day during the early evening. It was one of four Standard class 4s that moved to Tebay from Stoke in May 1967. It briefly survived the closure of Tebay depot at the end of 1967 with a move to Carnforth only to be withdrawn in February 1968. Some use was made of Clayton diesels from 1968 at Tebay after the Standard class 4s were moved away but apparently the need for banking up to Shap summit was much reduced from that time on.

Black 5 44886 plods up the 1 in 125 gradient at Thrimby Grange with a 24 wagon mixed freight and is approaching the bridge that carries the A6 trunk road. The train is near the end of a seven mile section at 1 in 125 that started after Penrith and has about four more miles of climbing before Shap summit. The approach to Shap summit for southbound trains, though not as steep as the northbound gradient from Tebay, was nevertherless a long and arduous climb. This was a tougher task for this engine than on 12th August when it had just three wagons to take over Ais Gill (see page 38). The structures beyond the A6 were part of Shap Beck Quarry from which limestone was conveyed by rail with a siding connection a kilometre beyond the bridge. This siding was used until 2014 when the Redcar steel works closed but is likely to be used again from 2017 with trains to Wigan.

FRIDAY, 19TH APRIL 1968   LANCASHIRE SHEDS

Showing off its shiny clean boiler and firebox, Stanier 8F No. 48400 poses between the turntable and the main 6 road shed at Rose Grove, originally a Lancashire and Yorkshire Railway depot. Built at Swindon in June 1943, 48400 had moved to Rose Grove from Carnforth in September 1967 and had previously been based in the East and West Midlands, Leeds, and in South Wales for trains on the Central Wales line. It was only withdrawn right at the end of steam in August 1968. Fourteen out of a class of 852 survived the cutter's torch but 48400 succumbed in December of that year. The black 5 in the background, No. 45096, had spent its entire post war life in the north west but had only been based at Rose Grove since the previous month.

Black 5 44845 stands in front of the water tank at Rose Grove shed. The tall building on the right is the coaling tower. Located on the western edge of Burnley, Rose Grove was one of only three sheds that stayed open until August 1968, the others being Lostock Hall (Preston) and Carnforth. The M65 now passes where the shed once stood. Apart from two months in Sheffield, 44845 was based in Manchester for all its post war life - at Belle Vue until that depot closed in 1955, then at Newton Heath until its withdrawal in June 1968.

Seen from the platform edge at Blackburn, 8F 48410 passes the station with a loaded coal train. The signals in the distance give no clue as to whether the train would turn left for Bolton via Darwen or carry straight on towards Preston. 48410 had been based at Rose Grove shed since December 1967 and survived until steam's last month, August 1968.

An unidentified grubby Stanier 8F at Bolton epitomises the run down of steam in 1968.

After bringing a mineral train from the Blackburn direction, black 5 44929 waits by a water crane outside Bolton depot, looking very smart on the outside and with a bright red buffer beam. Built at Crewe in March 1946, 44929 had moved to Bolton from Trafford Park in March 1968 having spent most of its post nationalisation life at Blackpool and Agecroft. It was withdrawn three months later in June 1968, the same month that Bolton depot closed.

Standard class 5 No. 73034 and an unidentified Caprotti valve gear fitted member of the same class stand nose to nose as sunshine streams in through the roof of Patricroft depot. 73034 had spent most of its fifteen year life based at Shrewsbury only coming to Patricroft in October 1966. It was recorded as being withdrawn during the previous month. The Caprotti fitted engine had probably been withdrawn also. Of the thirty in the class with this valve gear, twenty were withdrawn from service from Patricroft, twelve of them before April 1968 when this picture was taken, and a further three during the month. Four lived on until June 1968. The other ten spent most of their lives based at Glasgow's St Rollox shed.

Standard class 5 No. 73010 stands outside Patricroft depot, loco and driver ready for the next duty. 73010 was one of about a dozen Standard 5s on the shed that day, roughly half of all the engines there. Patricroft took an allocation of ten of this class in 1955 when brand new – numbers 73090 to 73099. Just over a decade later, however, Patricroft became the last home for no fewer than 45 members of the class mostly coming for short periods until withdrawal in late 1967 or 1968. 73010 was one of the last survivors and was withdrawn in June 1968. Patricroft shed itself was closed in July and was one of the last five steam sheds operating in the country.

Stanier 8F No. 48212 stands ready for action at its home depot, Patricroft. It had been transferred there from Northwich one year previously after being based at Westhouses shed near Alfreton and Hasland shed near Chesterfield for long periods before shorter stays at Toton, Leicester, Annesley and Aintree. It was withdrawn in June 1968. St Andrew's Church tower stands proudly in the background. Patricroft shed was adjacent to the line from Manchester Exchange to Liverpool Lime Street. Lyntown Trading Estate and the M602 occupy much of the former shed and sidings area.

Newton Heath depot three months before it closed in July 1968. There were still around 25 engines that day but maybe the empty sidings in the upper picture were symptomatic of the decline of steam and the end approaching. Opened in 1877 by the Lancashire and Yorkshire Railway, the shed was located some three miles east of Manchester Victoria between the lines to Rochdale and Oldham. Unlike Patricroft in the previous pages, Newton Heath remains in active railway use as a diesel maintenance depot.

SUNDAY, 11TH AUGUST 1968   SELSIDE AND KIRKBY STEPHEN
The last day of standard gauge steam locomotives on British Railways.

With Penyghent in the background, "Britannia" 70013 *Oliver Cromwell* heads north up the "Long Drag" shortly before 2pm with the "15 guinea special" at Selside, between Horton in Ribblesdale and Ribblehead.

Facing page. Upper: Seen at 16.40, black 5s 44871 and 44781 head the "15 guinea special" between Kirkby Stephen and Birkett Tunnel on the return journey from Carlisle.

Lower: Forty minutes after the black 5s, "Britannnia" 70013 *Oliver Cromwell* returns south at the same spot.

TUESDAY, 31 MAY 1966

For a parting shot, I deviate from the chronological order of the previous photographs back to my first day out photographing steam on the Settle – Carlisle line. This was the only time on my days out in North-West England when I saw one of the standard class 4s heading a train; on other days they were the pilot or banking engines for trains up to Shap summit. 75041 had the task of hauling just 19 wagons up from Appleby to Ais Gill summit, though some of those wagons look to have substantial loads. It was seen here approaching Dent Head probably on the way back to Skipton where it was shedded at the time. When Skipton depot closed in April 1967 it went to Carnforth until withdrawal in January 1968.